THE OFF-GRID LIVING GUIDEBOOK

ALVIN TAM

BAREFOOT SANCTUARY

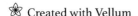 Created with Vellum

For my Wife, my Son, and the Earth

By discovering nature, you discover yourself.

— MAXIME LEGACÉ

INTRODUCTION

My wife and I started the process of escaping the city and moving into a forest over four years ago and now have lived in our completed off-grid house for over a year. There are constant tweaks and insights as to what we could have done better or differently, but overall, I'm beyond satisfied with how well our house is doing.

I didn't have any experience in building construction before I started this house. We moved to the forest without even a shovel. The most I had done in construction was helping my dad put up some drywall and cobbling together some wooden desks out of scrap wood when I was a teenager. The learning curve was steep but highly rewarding. It was worth every moment for me.

In fact my background didn't give me any experience in

building this house. I was a professional circus artist from the age of 18, performing for many productions around the world, including Cirque du Soleil, and then started a marketing and film production company in my mid-thirties. I was 43 years old when I started designing our house. Similarly, my wife is a yoga and dance instructor and circus performer, like me. Neither of us had construction backgrounds in the least but we did have a common dream of living in the forest.

———————

The Off-Grid Living Guidebook outlines the core components that were required for our successful off-grid build. I'll detail specifics on what made our particular design so that you can create a template to begin your build process.

What you'll gain from this guidebook is an overview of the entire process to help you begin to plan your project. In reality, each chapter could merit its own book or course, and you could spend years studying and practicing that dedicated trade. I want to share the process that I went through so that you can have a starting point for your off-grid dream house.

Building off-grid also necessitates a lot of numbers and

statistics. It's easy to get lost in the R-values, U-values, heat loss equations, kilowatt hours, and so on. I'll provide statistics at the end of each chapter about the most relevant numbers.

And in the end, the best message I can convey to you is to enjoy the process more than the result. It's something that, if I were to undertake such a big family project again, I would do differently. I charged ahead in my enthusiasm, and at times, forgot who I was building this house for and why. We're now settled into a nook in the forest, but it wasn't always easy and the struggles were very real. Don't forget your purpose, and stay connected to your loved ones around you as you build.

Happy Discoveries,

Alvin.

A day by the river.

1

OVERVIEW

PRINCIPLED LIVING

A principled approach to off-grid living is key to a successful final build. We'll take a look at how we approached our build, what we deemed necessary, and what we felt we could do without.

BUILDING DESIGN

We had a choice of many properties — why did we choose the one we live on? A review of the factors that determine an off-grid build, from the terrain, positioning for sun, proximity to towns or cities.

We'll also look at the planning process used to determine

the most efficient house design, why we planned the interior and exterior layouts and how it works in real-life situations. We'll also cover the regulatory process that was required for us to set up an off-grid home that complied with local bylaws and building inspections.

WATER SYSTEMS

Water is the key to survival: we'll review the steps we took to bring water to our home while minimizing the requirement for electricity to be used as a resource for moving water.

ELECTRICAL SYSTEMS

Our process in determining how much electricity we would need, and what we did specifically for our home's solar setup, wiring, and electrification.

HEATING AND COOLING SYSTEMS

Because of our extreme seasonal climates, we designed for cooling in hot Okanagan summers and heating for frigid Canadian winters.

Gathering water at a natural spring. This where we got most of our drinking water when we lived in the RV.

2
PRINCIPLED LIVING

OVERVIEW

1. Why Go Off-Grid?
2. A Mindset Change
3. Starting in an RV
4. The Act of Conserving

WHY GO OFF-GRID?

After having spent the majority of my life living in big cities, the last of which was Las Vegas, my wife and I felt that it was time for a change. We thought we were living a sustainable life. We operated a yoga studio in Las Vegas, conveniently located inside a Whole Foods Market, the largest retailer of organic food in the country. We had purchased a house in Las Vegas and put solar panels on the roof. We flushed, every 4 or 5 pees. We turned the lights out. We recycled. Hell — we even composted our organic waste, in the middle of an urban neighborhood!

And then it hit us. We had been running yearly yoga retreats in all over the world, and one year, we went to Peru. We brought 14 Americans to a quiet corner of Peru, in a region called the Sacred Valley, two hours from the famed Machu Picchu. On one excursion, we visited the local farmer's market. It didn't look like the plastic-wrapped market in Las Vegas (that was held in a shopping mall atrium). It was a display of bounty; fruits and vegetables, freshly picked and brought down from the mountainside that day. It was visceral, primal and refreshing.

It was time. And though we didn't know exactly what the final picture was going to be, we knew we had to take action. We headed north — to Canada. The rest is our journey — a template, a reference — a *guidebook* — for *your* successful, off-grid journey.

A MINDSET CHANGE

One of the first lessons I recall about sustainable living was a story about someone who was trying to live off-the-grid and complained that he didn't have enough solar power. How solar *just didn't work*. That he had to fire up his generator to keep the house running. That it was costing him more money than it was worth.

It turned out that this person was trying to live a life that was equivalent to one if you had unlimited electricity. The same appliances. The same electrical demands. The same wiring. The lesson that I learned from my solar provider was that **solar power is not a simple replacement for on-grid electricity but rather it's the first step in the change in mindset on the way you live.** But it turns out it doesn't mean living cheaply or in lack. It means that we designed our house differently from the beginning, with different considerations that shaped what we can do, and what we want to do. It means considering how basic assumptions about the way a house is built and operated need to be questioned and revised for your off-grid scenario.

STARTING IN AN RV

We didn't end up in an off-grid house from Las Vegas in one step. It was a long journey that took us from American suburbia to Canadian forest living.

After we moved to Canada, we stayed with acquaintances in their guest house for nine months. When we finally purchased our land, we decided to move onto the property as quickly as possible to save on further costs of rent. We had 18 acres of land after all!

This was the first step in learning about the off-grid lifestyle — and to see if we really could take it. We began our RV journey at the tail end of a long and cold winter. We had a very accelerated learning program on how to:

1. Operate power tools
2. Build an "add-on" shack to the RV to house a wood stove
3. Start fires in a wood stove
4. Melt snow to wash dishes
5. Buy generators
6. Take baths in a big Tupperware bin
7. Chop wood
8. Poop in a bucket.
9. Bum showers from friends

We stayed in the RV for two years while we saved up and planned the build for our off-grid house.

Off-grid living in an RV. Simple, but not easy.

THE ACT OF CONSERVATION

Living in the RV taught us about energy conservation. We had no facility hook-ups — no on-grid electricity, no gas feed, no water line. We started with a very simple solar power system — 2 panels and a single 12-volt battery. For water, we melted snow or collected rainwater, boiled it over the wood stove, and used it to wash dishes. For cooking, we used the wood stove or propane. None of the septic systems in the RV were used since we didn't have a way to prevent the pipes from freezing so we hand-carried out human waste, compost, and gray water in buckets to a tree or compost bin.

When we had to not only "ingest" resources (electricity, water, gas, food) but also pack everything out, it became very apparent how unconscious we had always been about using our resources. When your poop goes down the toilet, when the electricity comes from a power company, and water flows endlessly from a tap, it's hard to get a grasp on just how much you use.

We began to truly appreciate the act of conservation. It was no longer a vague notion in order to reduce a power bill at the end of the month. **Conserving resources meant that we wouldn't freeze that night, run out of water that day, or eat dinner in the dark if our batteries ran dead.** The idea of conservation became a very real set of behaviors in order to survive.

It was in this spirit of conservation that we began to plan and design our off-grid house.

BUILDING DESIGN

OVERVIEW

CHOOSING THE LAND

When we began the search for property in the country, we were faced with many choices. The main factors that went into the decision were:

1. Exposure to sunlight
2. Proximity to schools and amenities
3. Amount of land
4. Type of land (forested, farmed, waterfront)
5. The terrain of the land (flat, hilly, mountainous)
6. Cost

We already knew that we'd be powered by solar, so the south-facing exposure to sunlight was a key factor. Then, proximity to school was the next consideration as neither of us could imagine driving more than 20 minutes one-way to drop off our son. After that, it was about the type of land and the terrain.

We preferred forested land as we didn't have any intention of creating a farming business. And I wanted to explore the possibility of setting up a gravity-fed water system, so hills and elevation differences were also important.

After months of searching, we found an 18-acre parcel of land, 20 minutes from school, with south-facing exposure where most of the property slopes upward into a gentle mountain. The cost matched our available budget — and we jumped in headfirst.

We saw a lot of different properties during our search, and there were properties that I'm glad that we didn't try to buy. I'm glad that we held out and found what we were looking for and didn't settle for another piece of land because it was available sooner or slightly cheaper.

Initially, we had realtors take us to properties with an existing house. After having built a house from scratch, I'm very happy that we didn't try to buy a house and upgrade it. We were able to custom design not only the look and structure of our house but also design it so that it performs with maximum energy efficiency.

We also widened our search beyond our original geographical criteria. In other words, we ended up on a country road farther from the nearest city, five miles past the local town. It wasn't what I anticipated but it turned out for the best. Here are four reasons why I'm glad we bought the land that we did:

1. **The property came with a tested well.** I had no idea how important that was until I began hearing about all the horror stories of people

drilling wells and not hitting any water — and the associated, astronomical costs. The well was definitely a bonus that I overlooked.

2. **Proximity to a good hardware store.** We live 5 miles from the nearest town that has a pretty well-stocked hardware store and supplied the majority of my building materials. It turns out that you routinely forget the one thing you need to complete that day's worth of construction — the one tool, the one bag of screws, the extra piece of lumber. It was a huge advantage to be only 7 minutes away from building supplies. I highly recommend building close enough to a supply store so that you're not traveling a long time to pick up a bag of nails.

3. **Established trails on the property.** We bought the property with trails already cut through the forest. Originally, I liked this feature because we could enjoy walking through the forest without bushwhacking. This year, I realized an even more significant benefit — bringing up a truck so that we could log dead trees for firewood.

4. **Helpful neighbors.** It might seem obvious that having good neighbors makes living in the country easier, but it's an understatement. We've counted on our neighbors for everything: getting

towed out of a snowy ditch, borrowing a bobcat to leveling dirt piles, and washing loads of clothes. If it's possible, vet your neighbors before buying property to see if you can count on a local network for all the innumerable things you'll need help for.

FINDING A PLACE FOR OUR HOUSE

A few factors went into choosing an ideal spot for our house on our property. One of my main requirements was the proximity to the main road. We've been to places where the house was a winding drive up a mountain. While it's an amazing way to create the seclusion you might want, it also creates a host of other issues to deal with, like more snow removal to do in the winter, increased costs on creating or maintaining a long driveway and more difficult access for delivery of construction materials.

We put our house about 500 feet back from our country road and made a straight driveway right up to the house. While it lacks a bit of creativity for driveway entrances, it definitely made for easy delivery of our materials. The most notable benefit came when we had our roof trusses delivered — massive trusses that spanned the maximum allowable truck bed length and width. The truck itself was barely able to fit through our gate — but after it passed it was a straight shot up the driveway. It was the same story with concrete trucks and cranes.

The other consideration was to put the house on a flat area while finding enough slope around the house so that water would drain away from the house. Since we love trees, we tried to minimize the number of trees we had to take down (just one 60-foot pine) and chose a spot slightly up our hill. It provided enough elevation to allow water to flow down and away from our house.

The other factor we considered was using the natural shading of trees to reduce heating effects in the summertime. Since we only had to clear one tree, we used the trees on the west side of our property to block the late afternoon summer sun. By 4 o'clock most summer days our house would be partially or completely in the shade.

Would I do anything differently? Yes, if you can get farther away from fences or property lines, the better. There was the occasional complaint from our east-side neighbor about our garbage. Unfortunately, they are the exception to the community of awesome neighbors we've come to know. Also, if you want to add outbuildings or widen a driveway, you'll have room, instead of being right up against a property line.

DESIGNING A HOUSE

We made it! We had bought land, moved into an RV, and were living off-grid. We were ready to build a house. Now what? How do we begin? What things did we consider first?

For us, we had two main goals for the design of the house: one, it had to be maximally energy efficient, and two, it had to have enough interior space to hang a full-length trapeze! Besides being passionate off-grid adventurers, we are also professional circus artists and yoga teachers. So the goal of hanging a trapeze ended up greatly influencing and determining the final design.

The most energy-efficient shape of a building is a rectangle or a square as a quadrilateral presents the least amount of exposed wall. While it may not be the most creative design shape, I wasn't going after the aesthetics, so we opted for a 32-foot by 38-foot rectangle, with the shorter dimension as the front and back of the house. We chose these dimensions because that's what would fit on the landing that we cleared on the plateau on our hill. This is also why I recommend building away from a fence line if possible so that you can actually make your building footprint to the size you want and not be limited by setbacks (the minimum distance that regulatory building codes require you to build from).

To meet the trapeze requirement, I designed tall ceilings with an interior apex of 21 feet. The ceiling sloped down to the sides in a 30-degree slope, which allowed me to place additional anchor points next to the main central points.

Besides making sure we had enough height to rig a trapeze, I wanted to make sure that the roof was angled enough to allow snow and other debris to slide off, but not so steep that it would incur unnecessary effort (and therefore costs) to actually work on the roof. Based on my experience installing the trusses, laying down plywood and roofing membranes, and finally bolting together metal roofing panels, I wouldn't have wanted my roof to be greater than 30 degrees. We lost plenty of screws and the occasional tape measure slipping on the roof!

So in the end, our house turned out to be a basic rectangle with a triangular roof to cap it off. What about a basement or crawl space? We opted to not have either based on two reasons: it costs more and we reasoned that if we create more storage space, we're just going to fill it with junk. Our garage in Las Vegas was barely usable and it became a dumping ground for stuff we ended up selling or giving away when we moved. This design choice kept in line with our values of reducing material goods and aiming to live more simply. **While I'm not sure living off-grid is simple by any means, building with a reductionist attitude keeps what's most important in focus: doing our part, in whatever way possible, to contribute toward a healthier future world.**

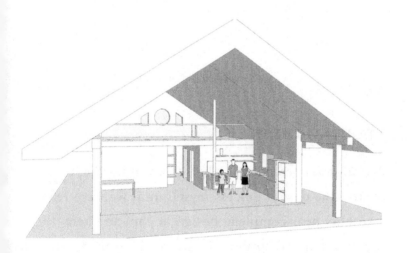

A 3D render of the front of the house and interior.

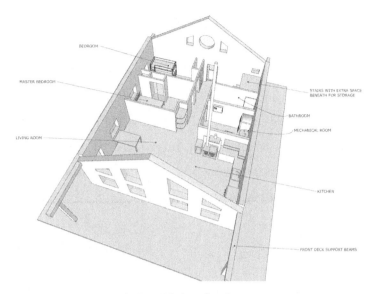

A 3D aerial view of our house.

STARTING THE DESIGN

A vital step in creating the house layout was being able to control the design process myself until we were ready to take the near-complete design to an architect to get construction blueprints. If we had worked with an architect from the very beginning, the cost of planning would have been a lot higher. As it turns out, we only paid about $1200 in architectural fees.

Because of my background in using graphic design and video editing software, I learned how to use SketchUp, a 3D design software, fairly quickly. SketchUp is used for just about anything that requires a simple but accurately-dimensioned digital mock-up. I had used SketchUp previously for some basic renderings but nothing as extensive as a house design. There's a bit of a learning curve and while it may not be for everyone to learn design software in order to build a house, I highly recommend it. It not only saved money, but it helped us configure the interior set up and then fly a virtual camera through the house. This phase of pre-visualization helped us make a lot of key choices that I think we would have missed had we not spent the time creating a virtual 3D design of our house.

The other advantage of creating a virtual 3D model of our home was to be able to share the designs with other people for feedback - family, friends, contractors. I got a lot more useful feedback when I showed people a 3D rendering of our design than a traditional two-dimensional layout drawing.

NAVIGATING REGULATIONS

We decided to build our new house to code and to meet all building standards, and in the end, we did just that. In fact we overbuilt the house in comparison to current day standards for insulation, water drainage, and structural requirements and ended up with a building that would perform efficiently for years or decades to come.

We had two choices: find a builder or become the builder. I wanted to have the experience of building a house because I had never done anything like it before. It was a DIY dream come true.

On the other hand, I had never built a house before, so the idea of spending thousands of dollars on a house — when my construction background was limited to putting up a few sheets of drywall when I was a teenager — was daunting.

In British Columbia where we live, I had to complete a two-day Owner Builder course and pass a test to get an authorization permit to build. There were a lot of people who didn't agree with this process (why should any agency dictate where and how I should build my house?) but I found it extremely useful since I had zero experience in building. At that time, I didn't even know which part of the build process came first — the rough-in plumbing or the walls? I was clueless.

I took the course in January and passed the exam in February. At the same time, I began designing the house in Sketchup. We received the authorization to build in

March and I began the process of assembling the permit application. We wanted our application process to be as smooth as possible, so I created a very clear and comprehensive package. This package comprised the following categories:

1. Permit application
2. Construction drawings
3. Truss and floor layout
4. Owner build authorization
5. Geotechnical review
6. Energy audit

All items were standard requirements in the BC application process except for the energy audit. I don't know if the energy audit helped with our application but it didn't hurt. In fact, it turned out to be the single most important step in the construction by conducting a blower door test that revealed energy-sapping leaks in our building envelope.

By the time we had our application approved and ready to go and all our contractors lined up, it was June and we were ready to start building.

As with most building inspection processes, we had 6-7 inspections along the way until our final inspection. We met the inspector with full transparency each time and offered as much information as we could each time. I know that we established a sense of trust with him from the beginning by submitting a well-organized and complete permit application package. It became a very important element to our successful build — being able to have the building inspector work with you, instead of against you, because he trusts your work.

DESIGN SPECIFICS

I've reviewed what the basic design turned out to be: a rectangular box with a triangular roof. In the design process, I also integrated these considerations into the final layout:

1. Length of overhangs for sun shading and weather protection
2. Position of open-able windows to allow for passive interior airflow
3. Placement of the hot water tank and bathroom and kitchen to reduce heat loss in hot water lines
4. Position of the mechanical room away from bedrooms to reduce noise
5. Placement of exterior doors to allow for efficient loading of groceries, furniture, bags

6. Size of interior doorways and hallways and room layouts to accommodate wheelchair or mobility challenged individuals

7. Position and size of windows to allow for maximum passive solar gain while reducing energy loss on the non-sunny side of the house

Let's discuss each specifically:

Length of overhangs for sun shading and weather protection. Now that we live in our house, it's clear that overhangs make a huge difference in the heating or cooling of the house. Our south-facing wall has a 10-foot overhang and it shades 90% of our front windows from the sun during the summer months. In the winter the sun comes directly through the windows all day on a sunny day and heats up our living space. The sides of our house are also exposed to the sun in the morning and late afternoon, so the overhangs are nearly 7-feet. This provides enough shade in the summer that only the early morning or late evening rays come in through the windows. The back of the house doesn't receive any sunlight at all so the overhang was a standard 2-foot overhang.

Overhangs also provide protection from the elements and create a more usable outdoor living space. Our particular design created about 8-10 feet of usable front outdoor space free from rain and snow. On the sides, since the overhangs are lower, we have nearly 6 feet of space. This winter shed a ton of snow — and the snow slid off the roof creating huge snow piles on the sides but still kept the bulk of the snow away from the exterior walls. We'll be adding a 10-foot overhang that covers the back of the house so that we can store wood and other yard tools.

Position of open-able windows to allow for passive interior airflow. We wanted to reduce the amount of electricity required to do anything — including moving air. In order to accommodate for airflow, we placed large bottom-floor windows on the front wall and smaller second-floor windows on the opposite wall, the back wall. The air comes in through the bottom windows, and then rises, and is sucked out the back windows. It's a combination of cross-ventilation (windows on opposite walls) and the stack effect (warm air rises out higher windows and pulls cool air through the lower windows). The only change I would make, now that we live in the house, is to increase the size of the open-able windows on our back wall that are higher. It would increase the stack effect and airflow on hot days.

Placement of the hot water tank and bathroom and kitchen to reduce heat loss in hot water lines. I wanted to minimize heat loss in our water lines and keep the plumbing as straightforward as possible. While I knew that I would source our plumbing to a professional, I figured I'd be helping where I could, or at least by keeping the lines minimal, it would decrease contractor costs and material costs. A recirculating heat pump can be used to ensure that hot water is present in the lines when you turn on the taps — but again that requires electricity. We ended up sandwiching the mechanical room between the bathroom and the kitchen, and while most houses feature multiple bathrooms, we went with just one.

Position of the mechanical room away from bedrooms to reduce noise. Early in the design process, someone told me to not share a wall between the mechanical room and a bedroom. We ended up placing the mechanical room, stairwell, and bathroom on one side of the house and the two bedrooms on the other side, separated by a hallway. In retrospect, it turned out to be a fantastic decision, as the sound of the equipment constantly turning on and off would be greatly annoying to anyone sharing a wall. We have two 24-volt DC water pumps that make quite a loud whirring sound, a heat-recovery-ventilation (HRV) unit that makes the dishes in our kitchen vibrate when on at full blast, the washing machine spinning, and the water softener running its cleaning sequence daily. Bottom line — keep the mechanical room separate from your quiet areas!

Placement of exterior doors to allow for efficient loading of groceries, furniture, bags. I've lived in many different places in my life, including second-level and third-level apartments. While the view was nice, I regretted the stairs every time I needed to haul ten bags of groceries, a piece of new furniture, or suitcases up three flights of stairs. On this build, I wanted to make sure that moving goods in and out of our house was effortless — meaning that everything was on a single level, from the car park to the kitchen and main rooms. We have a single back door and front door off to one side of the main living area. One of the most important design features is that we made the exterior doors 42 inches wide. It increased the costs of the doors by more than double — the standard is usually 36 inches but the extra width has made moving things in and out so much easier.

Size of interior doorways and hallways and room layouts to accommodate wheelchair or mobility challenged individuals. When we arrived in Canada, we stayed with an elderly couple in their guest home for several months. They lived in a beautiful country home but it had a basement, main floor, and second-level. The front door had a long set of wooden steps winding down to the driveway. It was a veritable landmine of obstacles for anyone who had a mobility issue. This couple had health problems and it was clear that their house was more challenging than welcoming. I wanted our place to be future-proof if we ever had problems getting around, or if we had a guest with mobility challenges.

Position and size of windows to allow for maximum passive solar gain while reducing energy loss on the non-sunny side of the house. An important passive design feature that is built into our house is the size of our south-facing windows and north-facing windows. To maximize the amount of sunlight that entered our house during the colder months, we placed 8 large windows that took up nearly 80% of the surface area of the south wall. In contrast, to minimize heat loss through windows on the north wall, we placed 5 smaller windows comprising approximately 30% of the surface area of the back wall. One note from experience: be prepared for a lot of light on sunny days during the winter months if you don't have built-in interior shades or curtains! We love the amount of light, but it can feel like you're suntanning on the beach...

Adding large south-facing windows for passive heating.

FOUNDATION

We decided from the very beginning that we didn't want to build in a basement level. Besides the additional cost, neither of us could think of any basement that ever lived in or had been to that didn't feel damp, crowded, or just crammed with storage and forgotten items. It seemed like a haven for collecting more junk, and our philosophy from the beginning was to do more with less. So we nixed the basement.

We chose to build the foundation with a foam and concrete product called insulated concrete forms — or ICFs for short. These interlocking foam blocks click together into place and stack just like Lego blocks. On the inside of the blocks are plastic strips that hold the two foam sides together. Metal rebar is laid upon these plastic strips. Finally, concrete is poured into the foam "mould" and the result is a highly insulated, extremely air-tight, nearly indestructible wall.

Many builders use ICFs for their foundation walls particularly if they have a basement. It offers structure, insulation and waterproofing all in one. Since we wanted to build our above-ground walls with ICF blocks, it made sense to start the foundation with them so we could simply continue a solid wall of foam and concrete all the way up to the rafters. It worked very well, as there are no breaks in the wall — especially not at ground level, where water can easily seep into the building through water build-up or constant rainfall.

The slab was a solid concrete pour that cemented our entire house together. Our builder insisted on laying rebar every 16 inches, so that the structure would be further solidified. We added a reddish pigment into the concrete so that the slab would be our final floor finish as well, reducing the need for a floor overlay like wood or tile. The most important feature of the slab was the radiant floor system, which is made of PEX tubing that is held in place in an insulated radiant floor heating panel, which I'll discuss in a later chapter.

Building our Lego house with ICF blocks. Our builder, Josten, and his endless creativity, were instrumental to our successful build.

BUILDING ENVELOPE

Almost every discussion I had about building an energy-efficient house, or came across in online forums, revolved around what the building envelope — or more specifically — the walls — were going to be made of. I tossed this question around in my head for a long time too and weighed costs, labor, and environmental factors. The choices for us came down to these ones in the end:

1. **Insulated concrete forms (ICF).** The ICF block proved to be the best solution for us as we had started the foundation with it. However, I was

trying to build a sustainable "green" home, and I realized that foam and concrete are two materials that are not naturally occurring (like wood), and that the production of these materials were not environmentally friendly. In fact, the production of Portland cement has a very high "embodied energy" factor. In other words, it takes a lot of resources to make concrete.

2. **Structural Insulated Panels (SIP).** SIPs are pre-built wall sections that sandwich a thick layer of foam between two panels of structural board, such as wood, metal, or magnesium oxide. Not only do SIPs provide high insulation values, but they are, as the name suggests, structural. This removes the need for traditional framing. And the panels generally come pre-built, so the on-site task is mostly in the assembly of the panels.

3. **Stick framing.** Stick framing is the tried and true method of so many of the houses we live in today — but there are tons of variations on the stick frame wall that can be built to high degrees of efficiency and air tightness. We explored creating a double wall out of 2x4 lumber, and sandwiching a layer of insulation in between, and another which used 2x10 lumber with a ton of

insulation between the studs and layers of
exterior foam to wrap the outside walls.

The more I researched wall assembly methods, the more variations (and pros and cons) I discovered. It was impossible to declare one system a winner, but the building instructor from my Owner Builder course told me that he would build his house with ICF, if he were to do it all over again. It made sense to me then and really makes sense to me now. Despite the high level of "embodied energy" in cement and foam, we ended up building a house that is extremely strong, air tight, keeps heat energy in in the winter and heat energy out in the summer. ICF is resistant to moisture as foam and concrete doesn't rot and repels bugs since insects won't burrow into the materials.

There are two areas of our walls that use a stick frame construction. The "gable walls" of our house (the triangular sections of the front and back walls) are stick framed. Building the triangular shape using ICFs and poured concrete would be too challenging, so we opted to build with traditional lumber. Those sections were made out of 2x10 lumber with plywood, a building wrap, and a 1.5-inch layer of foam on the outside.

ROOF

The roof became a very special consideration for us, as we had some specific design requirements to meet. Besides keeping the rain and snow out, we wanted a roof that could support human weight loads when suspended on it. As circus performers, we wanted to be able to hang trapezes and ropes from anchor points in the ceiling. The way our house is designed did not allow for a center post for structural support, so the final engineered truss design of our roof were sets of parallel chord trusses. On the trusses where we specified anchor points for human loads, the roof engineers doubled up the trusses and reinforced certain connection points.

We tied the roof together with blocking to prevent any tilting of the trusses. Instead of blocking the roof with only 1x4 lumber, we used long lengths of 2x6 lumber between trusses. Finally, we secured the roof structure together with ½- inch plywood.

It then came time to insulate the roof — and the gable walls. For this part, we again went with foam and hired a spray foam company to insulate. They arrived — in their hazmat suits — and sprayed 6-inches into the ceiling and 4-inches into our gable walls. On paper the R-value of foam is about R-7 per inch, so our roof has an approximate R-value of R-42.

I had never built a roof before, so when it came time to deciding what to put on the outside, I went with what seemed to be the most durable — and the most expensive. At the end of the book is a budget breakdown by percentage, and the roof was easily the most expensive segment of the build.

After we sheeted the trusses with 1/2" plywood, we lay down a waterproof protective membrane for ice and water. We used a brand by Iko, but there are many brands that make similar products. It turns out that I overspent and bought the extra durable membrane that is primarily used for roof valleys where you would see the most amount of snow and water collection but I wasn't disappointed as I know now that we have a very, very waterproof roof.

We then installed one of the more expensive parts of the build — a standing seam metal roof. Unlike a traditional sheet of metal that secured with the screw tops exposed, a standing seam roof has an edge that overlaps all the screws so that no tops are ever unprotected. A standing seam roof was definitely more expensive than most other options, like shingles or tiles, but it came with the comfort of knowing that it will last for decades with little to no maintenance.

Installing trusses with a crane.

WINDOWS AND DOORS

We didn't want to build a solid, windowless concrete bunker, although it was tempting to do so as the R-value would have been incredible! Our off-grid house has a lot of windows to let in natural sunlight and passive heating. The largest section of windows is our south-facing windows which let in the sun in the winter and are mostly shaded in the summer. We opted for triple glazed windows with argon-filled gas, which seemed to be the minimum requirement for an energy efficient house.

The doors were standard thickness doors, with double-pane glass for the inset windows, but we made the doors wider at 42 inches. I'm still grateful for this choice anytime we need to bring in groceries, supplies, and furniture.

The one window feature we spent a little extra on was a circular window on the back wall. It also came triple-glazed and it wasn't a significant expense more — but it is definitely an amazing feature to have in the house if your budget allows for it.

One interesting feature was how we addressed thermal breaks around the windows. A thermal break is an insulating material that prevents the transfer of heat through a conductive material, like metal or concrete. While we were preparing our ICF concrete walls, we set the positions and framework of the windows with wooden frames (window bucks). Since our walls are thick, we would have normally built a window buck for the window to sit within of 12.5 inches — the thickness of the wall. However, I was concerned about thermal bridging (the conductivity of a material to transfer heat out of our house). Wood is a poor insulator, and so we would have these window bucks all over our house moving precious heat energy out.

Our builder, Josten, came up with an ingenious idea: we

would build the window bucks in two sections — an interior frame of 9 inches and an exterior, removable frame of 3.5 inches. After we stacked the ICF blocks around the windows and poured the concrete, we removed the exterior frame and meticulously replaced the 3.5 inch space with leftover ICF foam cut to size! (I say "we" did the work, but it was my parents who ended up doing all the painstaking cutting and foaming.) The extra effort to create the thermal break around the windows was a ton of extra work, but now that we live in the house, I'm certain that the thermal bridging of a continuous wooden buck would have been noticeable.

INTERIOR LAYOUT

Designing the interior layout was like playing Rubik's Cube — every move affected another move. We drew and redrew the walls over and over again to finally settle on the design that we built. Here are a few factors that we considered during planning:

1. **Proximity of bathrooms and kitchen to the mechanical room.** I wanted to reduce the amount of heat loss and pipe used to move water from the water tank to the outlets, so we

sandwiched the mechanical room between the bathroom and kitchen.

2. **Handicap accessibility.** I wanted to make sure that, if we had a wheelchair or mobility-restricted person in our house, he or she would be able to move comfortably within our design. We roughly followed some disability standards such as wider doors and hallways. We ended up building in 36-inch doors (normally 30 or 32-inch) and a 48-inch wide hallway (normally 36-inches wide). We also didn't build any steps or inset floors anywhere, so the entire bottom floor plan is on a single grade.

3. **Position of the mechanical room relative to the bedrooms.** One of my first designs had placed the mechanical room next to a bedroom. In retrospect, this would have been a huge mistake. Since we don't have a basement to house the mechanics, our water circulating pumps, washing machine, inverter, and HRV all fit into the mechanical room. They all make noise and create vibrations on the wall. From softest to loudest: HRV, inverter, washing machine, circulating pumps. If a bedroom shared a wall, it would drive its inhabitants crazy!

4. **Size of bedrooms versus common areas.** We deliberately made the two bedrooms quite small,

in order to force us to spend most of our time in the common areas. We didn't like the idea of a large bedroom where one could easily hide out in; it was more important to we shifted the space to a larger area for our circus activities. In the end, our son turned the "living room" into a hockey play-space for him and his buddies!

5. **Limited storage space.** Yes, we intentionally did not design a ton of storage into our house. It sounds crazy, but our experience was that storage simply gets filled up with unwanted and unused items. When we lived in Las Vegas, we had a two-car garage and installed a wall-length cabinet with tons of storage. Within a year, it collected so much unused junk that we had to start storing stuff on the garage floor. It seems to me that possessions expand directly in proportion to how much storage you make available. We have small closets in each bedroom and one at the back door. For larger items, we do have an exterior shed to put things we use from time to time, or are used seasonally, like winter clothes.

6. **Expandable second-floor loft.** Because we opted for high 21-foot ceilings, it made sense to add the loft space above the rooms. This added another 500 square feet to our living space and opened up

the house for additional rooms. To future proof the space, we pre-installed plumbing for an extra second-floor bathroom (we ran additional toilet and hot and cold lines). We may never build more rooms upstairs, as we really like the open design, but the extra space is there if we need it.

7. **Thicker insulated walls between rooms.** We put in 2x6 walls between the rooms and stuffed them with Roxul (rock wool insulation). I didn't really want to hear my son snore!

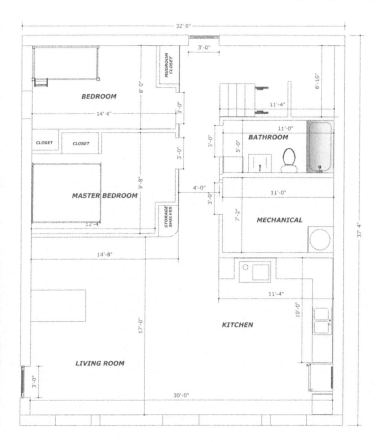

Layout of the bottom floor of our house.

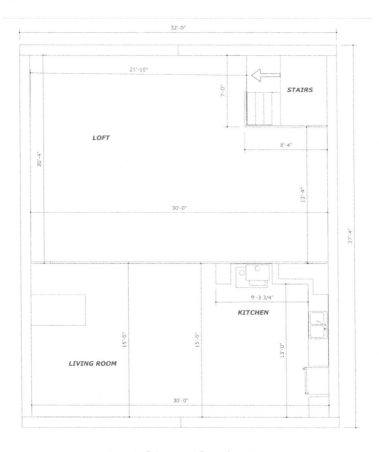

Layout of the second floor of our house.

BY THE NUMBERS

- Our house footprint is **32 feet wide by 37 feet long**. The south-facing wall is the 32 foot wall.
- Given that our walls are 12.5 inches thick, the actual livable interior square footage is 1100

square feet, plus a 550 square foot loft, for a total of **1600 square feet**.

- The highest point of our ceiling is 21 feet.
- The ICF blocks we used are manufactured by Amvic Building System. We used the Amvic 3.30 block which has an **R-30 value**. The foam is **3.25 inches thick** on each side, with a 6-inch concrete core between.
- Windows are measured in U-values and work inversely to R-values. The lower the U-values, the more insulative the window. We bought low-e triple-pane windows with argon from All Weather Windows in Edmonton, with a **U-value of 0.18.**

4

WATER SYSTEMS

OVERVIEW

WATER SOURCES

When we began our off-grid adventure in our small RV, I quickly realized that the single most important resource is water. We were able to get by without electricity — or at worse, we just fired up the generator if the solar panels were not charging the batteries quickly enough. We were able to get by without heat if necessary by bundling up with more blankets or my wife, my son, and I snuggling into the same bed. But there was no way to get by without water, and my experience in the RV taught me what an essential resource it is for basic health. Running water and a way to carry used water into a repository became the number one focus for me.

One of the most important aspects of the land we purchased was the inclusion of a dependable water source — in our case, a well. The well came with a specifications sheet with lots of numbers on it — but the most important details were the **well yield rate** and the **static water level.**

The well yield rate is the maximum rate at which a well can be pumped without lowering the water level. In our case, we were fortunate to have a well yield of 20 gallons per minute. We learned that other landowners had well yields of only 2-5 gallons per minute.

The static water level is how deep you need to drop your pump into the well before it hits the water. While our well is 167 feet deep, the static water is 73 feet. This number is significant because it determines the strength of pump we needed to order. Our choices were even more limited because we were doing everything off-grid. The deeper the static level, the more powerful the pump has to be, and we wanted to minimize the amount of electricity needed because we were going to operate the pump on solar power.

A side note: if you are looking at property with no well on it, make sure you do the testing on it first or check with neighbors on the accessibility to well water or other water sources. Drilling for water can be a very expensive task, and nothing can really start until a reliable source of water can be tapped.

We also have a small, three-season creek running through a corner of the back of our property. Many people have suggested that we tap this water source for domestic use or power generation. I haven't been keen on using it for a few reasons. First, it runs only intermittently from spring through the end of the summer. In the fall it reduces to a trickle and in the winter there is the risk of the stream freezing over. Secondly, it's easily 3000 feet from our house, so I would need to install and maintain a very long line of pipes — and if I wanted the water during the winter, I would need to dig a massive trench and bury a lot of pipe through some very beautiful forest. I wasn't willing to invest in the pipe and trench work and I definitely didn't want to disturb the natural forest with heavy construction. Finally, water sources have very specific water rights and we would have had to jump through a lot of official hoops to access this creek for domestic usage.

GRAVITY-FED WATER SYSTEM

One of the main questions I began with when designing our house was "how can we reduce the use of electricity everywhere possible?" When you have unlimited (or at least readily available) electricity, the solutions to problems default to electrically-driven machines (think electric can openers, pressure tanks, automatic coffee makers, hairdryers). I wanted to make sure that one of the biggest draws on electricity — the constant movement of water — was taken care of by an unlimited and free source — gravity.

One of the considerations that went into our land selection was having a hill or elevation to our property. This slope allowed us to plan for the installation of a water cistern part way up the hill to provide constant gravity-fed water. In electrically-driven pressure tanks, water pressure can drop from overuse of water or the water flow can be inconsistent if a pump needs to kick in. For our gravity-fed water system, the pressure is constant at all times, and the best part of all is that all our water movement uses absolutely no electricity.

But wait — how do we get the water up the hill into the cistern in the first place? We do use electricity to operate a water pump in the well but this process is done only when the cistern needs to be filled, which is every 15-20 days in the winter and every 10-15 days in the summer. And, in order to provide power to the pump, we installed a much smaller, independent solar panel system at the wellhead.

Installing a 1500-gallon cistern at the top of our hill for a gravity-fed water system.

The gravity-fed water system deserves its own step-by-step instruction manual, as it nearly rivaled the work of building a house. Having no experience in exterior plumbing, fluid dynamics, and water pumps, I am grateful that I went into the process mostly ignorant on just how much work it would take to install a gravity-fed water system that was powered by an off-grid, independent solar system. It took a lot of work.

Here are the steps we took to create an operational off-grid gravity-fed water system, once you have a well in place:

1. Determine the elevation of the water cistern to provide sufficient domestic water pressure (roughly 35 to 60 PSI or pounds per square inch)
2. Determine the size of the pipe needed to minimize pipe friction thereby reducing the need for a power-hungry pump and ensuring an adequate flow rate of water from the well up the hill into the cistern. Use a pipe loss friction chart.
3. Determine the size of the cistern by estimating your household water usage.
4. Determine the type of pump to use that works off a solar-powered DC-electricity source. We bought a pump from Grundfos.
5. Install a solar power system to power the pump.
6. Determine the "frost line" of your area, or at what depth the ground doesn't freeze in the water.

7. Dig a trench from the well to the cistern and install pipe, connectors, and frost-free hydrants.

8. Dig a hole for the cistern and install the cistern and access manhole.

9. Dig a trench for any branches of pipe from the main and install pipe, connectors, and frost-free hydrants.

10. Run the main pipe to your eventual house build.

11. Backfill all trenches and open cistern holes. Don't forget to backfill the first 6 to 12 inches of the trench by shovel, so that your excavator doesn't dump big rocks by accident onto the fragile pipes. This is work!

Installing the solar-powered well pump.

HOUSE WATER MAIN

We brought the water main line into the house during the foundation phase. We tested the pressure at the elevation at which we built the house, and it measured 37 PSI. Regular household pressure is about 40-60 PSI, so we were slightly below the norm. However, I like that our water pressure is not on the high end, as we save on the water we use because it doesn't blast out of our taps every time we turn on the taps. We may have to wait for an extra 30-seconds to fill our bathtub but that's a minor inconvenience.

We did a heavy metal test and determined that we needed a water softener. Our plumber also installed a filter, so all our incoming water is filtered and softened.

As for drinking water, we drink the water directly from our taps and are looking into installing a reverse osmosis unit to further purify drinking water.

OFF-GRID WATER TANK

Our hot water tank is the heart of the house and instrumental to living off-grid. It has to store enough hot water to be able to heat the exchange coils that run a loop into the in-floor heating system. The tank also has to have enough capacity to provide hot water for showers, dishes, and general washing if we don't have a fire going, or don't want to use the on-demand propane boiler. It also has to have multiple inputs for heating sources. A regular tank might use natural gas or electricity, but because of our off-grid objective, the tank had to be able to absorb energy from multiple sources.

We found the perfect tank — again at our local solar provider's store. The "off-grid" water tank was a behemoth of a tank with a volume of 120 gallons (residential tanks are usually 40 to 60 gallons), 4 inches of exterior insulation, and 4 separate inputs for hot water sources.

The tank is equipped to receive hot water from a gas boiler, a wood stove, and a solar thermal vacuum system, and an element for electrical heating. Currently, we have the tank hooked up to the wood stove, the propane boiler, and have pre-plumbed hot and cold lines from the outside into the mechanical room for a future installation of a solar thermal vacuum system.

The cost of the tank far exceeds a regular hot water tank (it was in the range of $4000-5000 Canadian). I debated in the beginning whether we should spend the extra money or just see if we could get by with a regular tank. I'm very happy we didn't skimp on the cost of this tank in the beginning — we would have had daily regrets for lack of hot water, inability to add heating sources, and loss of heat through inadequate insulation.

I knew that the tank had an electrical element feature, but I was doubtful that my photovoltaic system would be powerful enough to actually heat water. In the winters, it may be true, with all the gray days, but in the summers, the result is incredible. There is such a surplus of sunlight and energy, that it almost becomes necessary to divert the extra power somewhere — and what better place than to store excess electricity than as hot water? Leaving the element turned on for a few hours results in a nearly full tank of hot water, all from the sun.

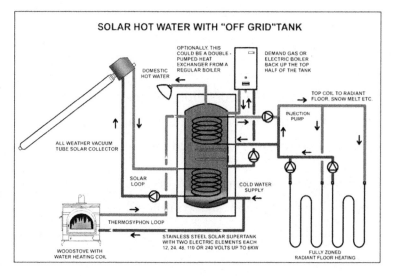

A diagram of the off-grid hot water tank with options for multiple heating sources.

SEPTIC SYSTEM

Before beginning our house build, I wasn't even sure what a septic tank was, so overseeing the installation of our septic system was an eye-opener. Again, we began with a septic consultant who designed our system for us. We ended up laying 200-feet of perforated white pipe, which comprises the septic field, then connected the pipes into a single distribution box called a "D-Box" (which is actually a cylinder in our case). The D-box is fed by another pipe that connects to the actual septic tank.

By the time we got to installing the septic tank, we had

some experience putting large cisterns into the ground, so I felt somewhat comfortable with the process. Using a small excavator, I dug a hole large enough to accommodate our 1000-gallon septic tank. Then, we chained the tank to the excavator bucket and lowered the tank into the hole and connected the pipes.

I had also done the majority of installing the wastewater pipes in the foundation, so I completed the septic system by connecting (gluing) the sewage output to the septic tank.

BY THE NUMBERS

- Our well has a yield rate of **20 gallons per minute.**
- Our water cistern holds **1500 gallons.**
- Our septic tank holds **1000 gallons.**
- The distance from the well to the water is cistern is **1000 feet.** We "teed" off a line from the main pipe to our house, then added another "T" to a hydrant by the garden, so the total length of pipe is nearly **2000 feet.**
- The type of pipe we used is called "muni pipe" — short for municipal pipe. This black pipe is rated

for higher pressure at 200 PSI. Regular below grade pipe for agricultural uses is rated at 100 PSI. I went with the muni pipe because I didn't want to dig up any broken pipes!

- The muni pipe also has an outside diameter of **1.5 inches**. Pipe diameter is referred to as OD: outside diameter and ID: inside diameter. The ID of the muni pipe we used is **1.25 inches**, and that is the number I used to calculate pipe friction loss.

- Calculating water pressure from gravity is a straight forward formula: divide your elevation in feet by **2.31** to obtain pounds per square inch, or PSI. The difference in elevation from the cistern to our house is 85 feet, so **85 / 2.31 = 36.8 PSI.**

ELECTRICAL SYSTEMS

OVERVIEW

POWER CONSUMPTION

It was important for us to test our power capabilities during the most challenging time of the year — the winter solstice. We moved into our bare-bones house in the middle of the winter when the windows, doors, and roof were installed — but not much else. It was a cold winter even though we had a roof over our heads as there were a lot of items left on the checklist: the doors needed to be sealed properly, the ventilation unit needed to be installed, and the in-floor heating needed to be activated. But our solar-powered — or photovoltaic (PV) system — performed amazingly. We were never short on power, our lights came on faithfully and our DC-powered fridge never stopped working. I even ran table saws in January!

We are fortunate to live close to someone I consider the most incredible off-grid resource possible. A lot of people sell solar but very few of them actually live off-grid and can attest to the effectiveness of their equipment. **Gillian Browning, owner of Sunfire Systems** in Lumby, British Columbia, is one of those rare exceptions. Not only does Gillian sell and install solar systems, but she has also been living off-grid herself for over 20 years on a mountain. She was the perfect guide for our off-grid adventure, and her store was based in the town where we moved! We were fortunate to consult with her from the beginning when our house was still in the design phase.

She helped us cultivate the mindset that living off-grid is not about sizing up a photovoltaic system to meet your current consumption, but instead looking at ways to adapt your lifestyle to minimize the need for resources (from electricity to wood to water) so that your daily footprint has the smallest impact possible. It was about looking at off-grid living holistically.

I began by asking myself what daily activities require electricity, and how can I reduce or eliminate the need for electricity to accomplish these tasks? Here is the list of daily activities I came up with:

1. Turning on lights
2. Operating a refrigerator
3. Cooking on a stove or oven
4. Using water
5. Heating water
6. Heating the house
7. Cooling the house
8. Washing and drying clothes
9. Powering and charging electronic devices
10. Powering household machines

AC VERSUS DC

Before we dive into the specifics of how we solved each of the above activities with a holistic off-grid solution, I want to highlight the single most important design feature we implemented into our house: **we wired the house to**

operate in both DC (direct current) and AC (alternating current).

Practically everything in our day-to-day lives operates on AC. An alternating current reverses direction a certain number of times per minute, giving us the standard North American 60 hertz per second. Most devices and household power consumption natively use AC — things like vacuum cleaners, blenders, lightbulbs, table saws, coffee makers and so on.

DC means that the current flows in only one direction, much like a battery. Almost all electronic devices, like cell phones, computers, and televisions, use DC.

Solar panels natively produce direct current, so the energy coming out of a photovoltaic system is DC. In order to change direct current to alternating current, an *inverter* is required. The problem with using an inverter is that a power loss occurs during the inversion. Depending on your inverter, the loss can be between 10-30%.

And since most electronic devices, like phones, tablets, and computers, natively run on DC power, a *converter* is required on the other end to change the AC power coming out of the wall into DC power that is suitable for your device. That's the "brick" that is on the power supply cable of your device or charging cable between the wall socket and your device. Another power loss occurs and more energy inefficiencies add up!

Our solution was to wire the house in both AC and DC systems. By code, we needed to install the regular AC sockets and circuits. But we went further by placing all the constant loads, like the lights, refrigerator, and pumps, on DC circuits. For our electronic devices, we installed DC plugs (similar to the cigarette lighter plug in your car) and found DC adapters for our computers and other 12 to 24-volt devices.

In the end, besides saving on our energy needs, having a house that operates on DC power helps us avoid the irritating hum of the inverter kicking on every time AC power is needed.

POWER SOLUTIONS

Now that you understand the background to economizing on electricity, let's take a look at the list of electrical requirements.

Turning on the lights. Lights can run on AC or DC. We installed a 24-volt DC system, so all our lights are high-efficiency LED lights that are designed specifically for

DC power. I didn't realize this distinction at first and nearly dropped a few hundred dollars at Home Depot on light bulbs. While DC-powered LED lights save us energy, they may have to be specially ordered as the availability and variety of DC lights are still fairly limited. I had to order specialty bulbs from China directly, so be aware that there is some additional upfront cost. We also minimized lighting energy usage by placing a lot of lights on different switches all over the house so that we could control the amount of lights and turn on only a few at a time or all of them if we needed bright lights.

Operating a refrigerator. One of the most consistent draws on electricity is the refrigerator. It cycles on and off, all day and all night. And when the power is low, there isn't an option of turning off the fridge until the sun comes back out, unless you're willing to throw out everything that has spoiled. In light of this challenge, we opted to go with a DC-powered fridge by Unique Appliances. I was aware that small fridges in RV's could operate on propane (and some on 12-volt DC power) but I didn't know that full size 24-volt fridges were available as well. We ordered a 13.3 cubic feet unit from Unique and while the initial cost of the fridge was much more than something you could pick up at the local appliance store, its efficiency is well worth the extra amount — the fridge doesn't even make a dent in our battery bank.

Cooking on a stove. It may seem obvious that a stove for an off-grid setup should be a propane stove (which is what we have) but it wasn't clear to me that I couldn't just go and buy a propane stove from Home Depot and install it. Traditional gas-fired stoves require a permanent electrical AC hookup to work, even if the fuel source is natural gas or propane. Obviously, that wouldn't work for us, so again, we were able to order a very proficient propane unit from Unique Appliances that ignited with a simple 9V battery. Since we heat the house in the cold months with a wood stove, we also end up using the wood stove (which also has an oven) to cook the majority of our meals.

Using water. When I was planning the gravity-fed water system, I thought that it would be a unique feature to our house because I would reduce power usage and guarantee consistent water pressure as long as the tank had water in it. I was right — we continue to experience these two benefits daily. But I didn't realize the full advantage of having a gravity-fed water system until our road suffered a power outage from a severe snowstorm. All our neighbors lost power for three days. Fortunately, most of them had wood stoves so they had a source of heat. But nobody could do anything with their water; take a shower, wash clothes, or flush the toilet. A few days of an un-flushed toilet is tough to deal with. We were the only ones on the road, to have lights *and* hot showers. I was extremely grateful that we opted for all the extra effort to build our gravity-fed water system.

Heating water. When electricity is abundant through a centralized power company, using electricity to heat water seems like an obvious choice. And in some rural areas where natural gas lines don't reach, electricity for heating water is sometimes the only choice. I wanted to make sure that our hot water options were flexible and not reliant on electricity.

In the winter, we burn logs in our wood stove to heat the house and cook our food. But while the fire is going, the stove also provides hot water. In the back of the wood stove is a water jacket — a coil of pipes that zigzags through the back of the stove, with an input for cold water, and an output for hot water. Both pipes are connected to a hot water tank and through the principle of thermosiphoning (heat rises, cold sinks) hot water begins cycling automatically into our tank. Within hours, we have 120 gallons of scalding hot water!

In the summer, since we don't burn wood, we divert excess solar energy into an electric water element. Currently, I manually switch on the element when the sun is out and in full force, and we plan to automate the energy diversion in the coming years, so that the element automatically turns on when power absorption reaches a certain peak. We also pre-plumbed lines for **solar vacuum tubes** which are tubes that house a thin column of water surrounded by an airless vacuum. In a vacuum, water boils at a much lower temperature than 100 degrees Celsius. The tubes collect the energy of the sun and exchange the heat with a glycol filled pipe. The pipes run back into the house and through a heat exchange coil transfer the sun's energy into the hot water tank. Instant hot water! We hope to eventually install these solar vacuum tubes but there is, like all our off-grid systems, a considerable upfront cost.

Heating and cooling the house. When I began designing the house, the number one question was, "What is the R-value of your walls, roof, windows, and so on?" Once I began the build process, it became apparent to me that there was so much more to the overall energy efficiency of the house than a singular R-value number. There was air tightness, window to wall ratio, overhangs, whether or not you had a wood stove with a chimney (a constant hole in your house), dryer vents, fan exhaust vents, and whether or not you keep forgetting to close the door or windows. When it came down to it, I tried to reduce energy used to heat and cool the house by designing a proper building envelope.

As mentioned in the *Building Design* section, we aimed to use the most insulating materials that were within our budget in our building envelope (the walls, floor, roof, windows and doors). We decided on 2 inches of sub-slab foam with radiant floor heating, an ICF block for the walls with 6.5 inches of foam, and a 6 inch spray foam insulation. Our stick-framed walls had 1.5 inches of exterior foam insulation and 4-inches of interior spray foam. The windows were triple-glazed, and the doors were regular exterior doors, but just on the wide side at 42 inches. Here's how it all measured out, when you attached R-values to the materials:

- Sub-slab (foam panels): R-14
- Vertical walls (ICF blocks): R-30
- Gable walls (spray foam and exterior foam panels): R-33
- Windows (triple-glazed with argon gas): U-value 0.18 US

Practically, the experience is what's most important. Our heating needs are almost entirely taken care of by the wood stove and the use of our heat recovery ventilation unit (HRV). The wood stove burns hot and the HRV moves the hot air around. The radiant in-floor heating system works well also, but we've been fairly content with the wood stove as our primary source — so far. We live in the interior of British Columbia, so obviously your heating and cooling needs will vary with the climate you're in. Our winters range from 0°C to -15°C, so we don't have excessively cold and windy winters. As a backup heat source, and in order to pass building code, we also have an on-demand propane boiler that quickly heats up water for our in-floor heating system (or really long showers).

Our cooling needs are negligible also — the hot summer months don't seem to heat the house much unless we leave the front door wide open to bring in the summer air. While the day is hot outside, the house stays cool all day. We can also activate the HRV to circulate our earth-tube-cooled air. Finally, we have the windows positioned to create a natural interior airflow effect — large open windows at the bottom of the house allow air in and flow up and out to windows on the opposite side, near the top of the walls.

Besides the insulating quality of the building envelope, the second most important passive building features are the overhangs. We weren't sure how big to make the overhangs until I had completed the general house design in Sketchup and discovered that I could geo-locate the model by entering actual latitude and longitude coordinates. The software could then position the sun and create shadows on my model so that I could actually see where the light entered the house. This process was key in positioning windows and designing the size of the overhangs. In the end, our front overhang is 10-feet deep and our side overhangs are 7-feet deep. The result of the overhang design is that hardly any sunlight enters through our south-facing windows during the very hot summer months, and all the sunlight enters our house in the winter months. It's almost a little too bright that we nearly need sunglasses inside in the winter!

Washing and drying clothes. I knew that washing clothes would be a regular electrical load and thought about this task a lot. In fact, while we were in the RV, and of course didn't have a washing machine inside, I ended up ordering a foot-pump washing unit! Unfortunately, I didn't realize that it was a new product in development and by the time it arrived from China, I had finished building my house. It'll be something I take out on a rainy day (literally if the batteries aren't charged because it's cloudy)!

There are no DC-powered washing machines that could accommodate a regular size load of laundry, so we went with the most efficient washing machine we could find, an LG unit. When we need to do laundry, and if we're hitting lower levels on the battery banks, we'll wait for a sunny day. This results on occasion on a few days of backed up dirty laundry which is a minor inconvenience. However, on sunny days, or just bright days with light cloud cover, our PV system provides plenty of power for washing clothes.

Drying clothes is a different story. Many dryers are electric-based machines, and using electricity to heat or dry anything is a huge electrical draw. Propane dryers are available, but I wanted to reduce our dependence on fossil fuels, so we went the most economical, ecological, and old-fashioned way possible — we hung our clothes to dry inside. So far it has worked every time without a fault — the clothes always dry!

Powering and charging electronic devices. The use of computers and phones was key since our business and all our communications runs off computers and phones. Our off-grid situation called for a more planned approach since we wanted to minimize power loss on as many levels as possible.

As mentioned, solar panels produce DC-power natively, so inverting DC to AC, then converting AC back to DC to use in our electronics is a very, very inefficient way to use our precious solar power — which is why we wired our house with parallel DC circuits throughout. Next to our regular AC wall sockets are DC sockets. These sockets have the same cigarette-style plugs you still see in cars and outputs 24-volts.

The problem is that most electronic devices don't run natively off of 24-volts, so a converter is required to step down the voltage to the required levels. Here's a list of what some of my electronics require:

- Macbook Pro: 19 volts
- LG computer 27" monitor: 19 volts
- Phone charger: 5 volts

We don't have a widescreen television but the larger units have AC wire inputs only, as the converter is housed on the inside of the units and you wouldn't be able to connect it to a DC wall socket.

I was able to find a company in California that manufactures DC to DC converters with a switching box that allows you to set the desired output voltage to your device. They happened to have a 24-volt input box that output to 12, 15, 16, 18.5, 19.5 20 and 24 volts. It was perfect for our situation and though the converters are a bit on the pricey side, it's well worth the money knowing that I'm not wasting power by inverting and converting my energy just to charge a cell phone or power up my computer.

Powering household machines. We didn't want to build a house that was so restricted that we couldn't use normal appliances. Fortunately, the way our PV system is sized allowed us to power just about any regular AC machine for a short period of time. We have run vacuum cleaners, high-powered blenders, commercial floor polishers, table saws, and construction work lights using only our solar system. The main difference is that our energy supply is limited, especially on cloudy days or at night, so the use of these power hungry devices can only be intermittent and short in duration. I rarely felt limited, however, in the use of these devices, because I don't need to run my blender or table saw for more than a minute or two at a time.

That said, there are many other machines that deliver modern convenience — microwaves, coffee makers, and huge televisions — that you may have to learn to live without. So far, we don't really miss anything, because our real needs are provided for, and there's nothing more satisfying than knowing that we won't ever have another electricity bill for as long as we live in this house.

PHOTOVOLTAIC SYSTEM

Before building the house we had some limited experience with living on solar — our off-grid RV living adventure taught us that power is precious! For our RV, we bought 2 solar panels and used the existing 12-volt car battery with a very simple charge controller. While we didn't have huge electrical needs inside the RV, cloudy periods or short daylight winter days made for many a time when we lit up candles instead or powered up the generator to get a few more minutes of computer work time in. Again, living on a small system taught us to be economical with our power usage, and turning off the lights was more than just a good habit to save a few dollars on the monthly power bill; it was an essential habit that had very real repercussions.

When Gillian designed the system for our house, we decided to oversize it for what we anticipated our actual needs would be. Here are the actual components of our photovoltaic system:

- 16 x 300-watt Canadian made **solar panels**
- 1 x Magnum 4000-watt **inverter**
- 2 x PT-100 Magnum 100 amp **charge controller**
- 12 x Rolls Surrette 2-volt **batteries**

- Plus all the usual wires, breaker boxes, connectors

A very simple overview of how a PV system works is as follows:

1. Light from the sun is gathered by the **solar panels** and converted into electrical energy.
2. The electricity passes through a **charge controller**, regulates the outgoing electrical signal and keeps it constant.
3. The outgoing electricity charges the **batteries**, or if the batteries are fully charged, is passed on to whatever electrical load is required.
4. The **inverter** changes DC electricity to AC electricity.

Sixteen solar panels power our off-grid house.

There are questions that I am asked repeatedly: do you get enough power in the winter? What about those long stretches of snowy, gray days with shortened daylight? Can you generate enough power to survive those periods?

Well, we discovered that, despite a 3-week period of cloud and snow during the winter solstice, our batteries never dropped below 50% capacity. It was amazing to see that we had power to run all our basic needs, like lights, the fridge, and electronics.

That said, it was important to time the use of more power-hungry appliances, such as the washing machine. We would wait for sunnier periods to run our loads.

Living off-grid doesn't mean matching an on-grid lifestyle's demands by amping up batteries and panels. It means understanding where the limits of your resources are, and living within them. It means adapting to limited resources by changing the timing of your wash, turning off all the lights, reducing the use of the electronics or other powered machines.

And, if you really must use power, you can always fire up a generator. We turn on our generator a few times in the winter as a precaution to top up the charge on our batteries and to run a few machines like the washer and power tools.

BY THE NUMBERS

- Our off-grid refrigerator operates on **24 volts and holds 13.3 cubic feet.**
- On a cloudy winter day, our panels still output **120 to 130 volts** of power.
- We have **twelve, 2-volt deep cycle batteries,** connected in series to create a 24-volt system.
- In addition to the regular AC plugs, we installed **12 DC plugs with USB outlets.**

HEATING & COOLING SYSTEMS

OVERVIEW

1. Heating Options
2. Wood Cook Stove
3. Propane Boiler
4. Earth Tubes
5. Heat Recovery Ventilation (HRV)
6. Door Blower Test
7. By the Numbers

HEATING OPTIONS

We knew that the wood stove was going to be a central piece in the off-grid puzzle. We already had experienced two winters living in the RV and knew that we couldn't survive without a reliable heat source. There are many different ways to heat your house and we looked at multiple options before making a decision. Here are a few that we considered, and the pros and cons from our point of view:

1. **Wood stove.** A traditional wood burning stove with a front-loading door. *Pros: Charm of an interior wood fire, can cook on the stove top. Cons: Relatively inefficient wood burn compared to an exterior wood boiler or thermal mass stove, smaller fuel loads, no thermal mass to capture and retain heat, messy load and clean up.*

2. **Wood cook stove.** Similar to a traditional wood burning stove except for additional features, such as a water jacket, stovetop, and oven. *Pros: Designed to cook or bake, includes an approved water jacket to heat water into a hot water tank, charm of an interior wood fire. Cons: Same as a wood stove.*

3. **Masonry heater or thermal mass stove.** Much like a wood stove but designed with a thick envelope of "thermal mass" - usually stone, brick or clay that stores and slowly releases heat energy. *Pros: Maximizes on a wood fire by capturing immediate heat in the thermal mass. Cons: Large*

interior footprint, usually doesn't have a cook-top, or come necessarily with a water jacket.

4. **Exterior wood boiler.** A highly insulated and efficient wood burner that is installed outside. A small pump circulates water into and out of the house via buried insulated pipes. *Pros: Incredible burn efficiency due to a highly insulated container, exterior loading of wood and cleaning of ashes keeps mess outside, long burn times compared to wood stoves due to higher wood load volume. Cons: requires electricity to run the circulation pump, lacks the charm of an interior fire, high initial purchase and installation cost.*

5. **Propane boiler.** An on-demand water boiler that uses propane. *Pros: Instant hot water. Cons: Burns a fossil fuel, propane is expensive, requires electricity for circulating pump and boiler, depending on the type of unit.*

6. **Solar vacuum tubes.** Water-filled tubes inside a cylindrical vacuum with an in-built heat exchanger converting the sun's energy directly into heat. *Pros: Uses the sun's energy to directly capture heat energy, effortless except for a low voltage circulating pump (also solar powered), little to no maintenance, no fuel requirements! Cons: High initial*

purchase and installation cost, heat produced is limited to availability of sun.

7. **Solar electric.** Converting the sunlight into electrical energy through a traditional photovoltaic system and then powering an electrical heater to warm air or water. *Pros: No moving parts — no maintenance, no fuel costs ever! Cons: Requires significant sunlight to produce enough electricity to power electrical heating elements.*

8. **Geothermal.** Installing pipes deep into the warmer-than-surface-air earth, circulating glycol, and transferring the heat into the building. *Pros: Potentially an infinite and constant supply of heat from the earth, completely non-polluting. Cons: Uses electricity to circulate heat exchanger, high initial cost and installation.*

9. **Gas or diesel generator.** Running a gas or diesel powered generator to electrically heat air or water. *Pros: Instant power allows for rapid heat generation via electrical air coil or water heating elements. Cons: Expensive, loud, polluting.*

WOOD COOK STOVE

We opted for a simple wood cook stove — an approach that would provide the heat that we needed, while eliminating the need for power to operate the unit, and have the necessary, insurance-approved features to connect to our hot water tank. The water jacket became a key deciding feature because we wanted to be able to heat our hot water tank using *thermosiphoning*: the process of water self-circulating from the natural effects of hot water rising and cold water sinking.

The water jacket is a coil of pipes in the back of the stove that absorbs heat. An incoming pipe brings cold water, and an outgoing pipe carries hot water to the tank. The hot water naturally rises, and if a tank is placed appropriately within a close distance, and *higher than* the pipes on the stove, thermosiphoning will occur. The hot water enters the tank at the top, and begins to cool. As it cools, the water sinks to the bottom cold water output pipe. The cold pipe angles down to the stove, so the cold water naturally flows down to the water jacket. The whole process repeats — and the most amazing thing is that it requires ZERO electricity!

I learned about thermosiphoning from videos and articles but wasn't sure if it would work. After all, most non-municipal plumbing solutions today use pressure tanks or electric pumps to move water through hot water tanks. Fortunately, my plumber had installed several hot water tanks and connected them to wood stoves, so it became a matter of calculating the optimal height and distance away from the hot and cold water pipes of the wood cook stove.

I discovered that the optimal arrangement for a wood stove and water tank would be for the tank to be directly above the wood stove. The hot water would rise vertically, without little to no horizontal displacement. However, since I was not placing my hot water tank on the second floor, I needed to make sure that the slope of the hot water pipe was not so gradual that the hot water would rise naturally on its own. The rise over run is 1 in 20 — in other words, for every 20 inches of horizontal pipe, it must rise at least 1 inch.

In the end, I designed the hot water tank to go directly behind the wood stove, on the other side of the wall that separated the kitchen area and the mechanical room. In order to set up a successful thermosiphon loop, the rising hot water pipe must have no high points, then low points. In other words, the hot water pipe into the tank from the stove must always rise, never plateau, and certainly never angle back downward. The same is true for the cold water pipe — the output from the tank must slope continuously downward to the wood stove.

The actual result is amazing. Our wood cook stove

provides heat for warmth, a source to cook or bake our food, and an automated hot water source! In the cold winter months, when we light a fire for the better part of the day, our entire 120 gallon tank is completely full of very, very hot water. For safety, as in all water tanks, a pressure relief valve is installed.

The heart of our home - a thermosiphoning wood cook stove.

PROPANE BOILER

In order to pass building code, we needed a heat source that could be operated independently and automatically. If we needed to close up our house in the middle of winter and leave it for a few weeks, we needed to show that the house would have its own heat source and the interior would not freeze.

We went with a newer on-demand propane boiler and connected it to our off-grid water tank. The entire system is tied together with a 24-volt DC thermostat. The heating process works as follows:

1. A thermostat measures the air temperature.
2. When the temperature drops, the thermostat turns on the pump that circulates the in-floor heating.
3. An aquastat (or temperature probe inside the water tank) measures the water temperature.
4. If the temperature drops below a certain limit, it turns on the pump that circulates water to the propane boiler.
5. The boiler is activated by water pressure, so once the pump starts moving water, the boiler fires up.

6. Once the idea water temperature is reached, the pump stops, and the boiler also stops.

7. Alternatively, if the wood stove is lit and sufficiently heating the water tank, the boiler will not activate.

As a note, we'll likely be adding solar thermal heating in the future, as it works when the sun is out or on bright cloudy days, even in cold weather. My personal goal one day is to heat our house without burning anything — propane or wood. It's a high reaching goal, but it's a question of combining heating sources that are naturally produced, such as solar thermal, solar electric, or perhaps one day, geothermal.

EARTH TUBES

One of the main features I wanted to include in our off-grid house was the integration of "earth tubes". A tube or pipe is buried underground with one end going into the house and the other end exposed to the outside some distance away from the house. The purpose of an earth tube is to bring outside air into the house by first conditioning the temperature of the air via the underground portion of the tube. In the winter, underground temperatures are more constant, so the outside air warms up. In contrast, air that passes underground in the summertime will cool down, so the air entering the house is already at a cooler temperature.

The tubes we used are 6-inch "Big-O" pipes — large corrugated flexible exterior piping — that we buried 7-feet underground. We buried 4 long sections of tubes at 100-feet each, and combined the air intake into a single input, which we connected to our HRV (heat recovery ventilation) unit. On the other end, the outside end, the tubes were brought back to the surface and stuck out above ground. We secured mesh and metal grills to the ends of each tube and built a small boxed shelter around the pipe endings to keep snow, water, dirt, and animals out.

Because every bit of fuel we use to heat our home counts, whether the fuel is wood or propane, I wanted to make sure we were tempering the outside winter air with the earth tubes first. When the outside temperature is 3°C, the incoming air, after winding through 400-feet of tubes 7-feet below the ground, is 11°C. It's a net increase of 5 to 8°C with absolutely no use of fuel or power.

In the summertime, it can be used in reverse to cool the house. The earth tube system is simple, functions with no power or attendance, and over time adds up to huge heating and cooling efficiencies.

Laying 400 feet of Big 'O pipes for our underground earth tube system.

HEAT RECOVERY VENTILATOR (HRV)

There are many ways to bring air and heat into your home. We went with a unit called a heat recovery ventilator, or HRV. The HRV brings exterior air into your home, while exchanging the incoming supply with the outgoing interior air. Through a heat exchange core, approximately 80% of the heat energy is conserved and transferred to the incoming air, minimizing energy loss. In a traditional forced air system, inside air is simply cycled out.

Our HRV is a Panasonic model that, on paper, sported the most efficient uses of electricity. It would be, besides lights and the fridge, one of the machines that would require a constant supply of electricity.

BLOWER DOOR TEST

If someone asked me what was the single most important thing we did to ensure the energy efficiency of our house, I would say that it was the fact that did a blower door test. From the start, we began working with Nick Watson, an energy efficiency advisor. He helped us create a virtual energy model of our house by determining how various R-values, building envelope materials, layouts, and doors and windows would affect the efficiency of our house. It was key to our planning process — from how we decided on creating a basic box for our house to how to chose various building materials, like ICF blocks or spray foam insulation.

But the most important part of the energy efficiency process happened with the blower door test. When we had the walls up, roof on and spray foamed, and doors and windows installed, Nick came back to do his test. At this point, the drywall was still not up, and all the various door and window perimeters were not fully sealed. Nick closed the front door and sealed off the back door with a nylon covering that had a fan in the middle that was connected to his computer software. The blower door test blows air into the house and then measuring its interior pressure revealing air tightness in air changes per hour, or ACH.

Our initial test yielded an ACH of 1.3, which isn't bad for a house — but wasn't close to the passive house standards of 0.6. I was determined to find the leaks so Nick reversed the fan, drawing air out of the house. We ran around the house with a can of spray foam looking for leaks. After 20 minutes, and half a can spray foam used up, we retested, and came in a 0.9 ACH.

These numbers are incredibly significant: with a few minutes of time and a few dollars of foam, we essentially increased our energy efficiency by over 30%, which translates into a direct savings of energy for the lifetime of our house. Had we simply put up the drywall and forever covered up the leaks, we would be spending a lot of extra energy and effort heating or cooling this house. It was an incredibly simple and straightforward test that I can't recommend enough if your goal is to build energy efficient.

BY THE NUMBERS

- For our earth tube system, we installed **400 feet of 6-inch "Big O" pipes, 7 feet underground.**
- Thermosiphoning works when the pipes rise **1 vertical inch every 20 horizontal inches.** The more rise, and less run, the better, so that the water moves more quickly through the loops.

7

BUDGET BREAKDOWN & TIMELINE

One of the most common questions is: how much did it cost? To answer: overall costs will be determined by cost of material and labor in your area, so, rather than provide actual numbers which may fluctuate anyway, I've included a breakdown by percentage. During the build, I recorded expenses according to the build phase so I could stay on budget but also so that I could get an idea of how much each phase would cost.

1. **2% — Design and Permitting:** architectural design, engineering, geotechnical engineer, permit applications
2. **1% — Site Preparation:** portable toilet rental, site clearing, site marking
3. **3% — Septic System Installation:** plumbing

material, drain rock, excavator rental, septic tank and accessories, labor

4. **15% — Footings, Foundation, Slab:** footing forms, concrete, ICF blocks, PEX insulating panels, PEX tubing, rough-in plumbing, rough-in electrical, radon rock, excavation, labor

5. **10% — Walls:** ICF blocks, concrete, window bucks, stick framed gable walls, house wrap, silver insulation boards, labor

6. **18% — Roofing:** truss design and manufacturing, front post and beam overhang support, truss bracing, plywood sheeting, crane service, metal roofing, flashing, labor

7. **6% — Doors & Windows:** doors and windows package, window wrap, lift rental, spray foam, labor

8. **12% — Electrical:** wiring, lighting, switches, 16 solar panels, charge controllers, inverter, labor

9. **5% — Interior Framing:** floor joists, lumber, labor

10. **11% — Plumbing & Mechanical:** finish plumbing, bathroom, kitchen fixtures, wood stove installation, hot water tank, propane boiler, pipes, HRV, ducting, labor

11. **5% — Drywall & Wall Tiling:** drywall, tile, labor

12. **5% — Appliances:** fridge, wood stove, washer, range hood, water softener
13. **2% — Interior Finishing:** stairs, window trim, door trim, baseboards, guard railing, paint, labor
14. **5% — Exterior Finishing:** fibre cement boards, chimney flashing, boom lift rental, scaffolding rental, pine soffit material, laser rental, labor

TIMELINE

I didn't really have any sense of how long it would take to build a house, so we just went as fast as we could take it. We were quite motivated to get the house together — we had been living in our RV for over a year and a half and were ready for more space. I also like the feeling of completion without leaving projects half-finished.

Pre-Construction Phase

It took about 1 month to design the house and come to a near-final look. The rate of design was accelerated because I was able to quickly modify layouts in Sketchup and then render a new plan and 3D model to get feedback from my family and other contractors. Having the ability to edit my own designs on the fly was a huge asset in building this house.

After we settled on a design, we ended up waiting for a few more months before the weather and contractor availability lined up to start building. During these months, we assembled the building permit, which took several weeks of focused work. When we finally received the permit to build in May, we were ready to start.

Construction Phase

Here is the timeline that we took from initial excavation to locking up the house. We didn't want to spend another winter in the RV, so we really pushed to get in before winter set in as we broke ground in June.

1. Day 1: Break ground, site preparation
2. Day 5: Excavation
3. Day 14: Earth tube installation
4. Day 16: Footings and concrete pour
5. Day 24: ICF foundation installation
6. Day 30: Foundation concrete pour
7. Day 42: Sub-slab plumbing and foundation backfill
8. Day 45: Radiant floor installation
9. Day 51: Slab concrete pour
10. Day 59: ICF wall construction
11. Day 67: Deck foundation excavation
12. Day 85: Interior framing

13. Day 92: Truss installation
14. Day 104: Roof sheeting and protective membrane
15. Day 128: Electrical rough-in and solar panel installation
16. Day 140: Windows and door installation
17. Day 149: Roof spray foam and metal roof installation
18. Day 171: Drywall
19. Day 200: Wood stove installation and finish plumbing

After we were able to lock up the house, we relaxed in the timeline, and spent the winter months painting the walls, adding window trim and baseboards, and building custom interior doors and stairs. In the spring, we sided the house with fibre cement board, which in itself was a two-week process.

8

RESOURCES

PEOPLE

- SOLAR POWER AND OFF-GRID SYSTEMS: Gillian Browning, Sunfire Systems, www.sunfiresystems.ca
- ELECTRICAL AND SOLAR INTEGRATION: Tim Brassard, Electric Ninja, www.electricninjaokanagan.com, electricninja3@shaw.ca
- OFF-GRID BUILDER: Josten Goulding, BlueDog Building Co., josgoulding@gmail.com
- OFF-GRID WATER SYSTEMS: Mike Visscher, I-Plumb, mike.visscher@gmail.com

- OFF-GRID WATER TANK AND SOLAR THERMAL: Patrick Spearing, patrickspearing@gmail.com
- OFF-GRID ADVISOR: Mike Reynolds, Ecohome.net
- ENERGY ADVISOR: Nick Watson, EnviroMez, www.enviromez.ca, nick@enviromez.ca
- EARTH TUBE ENGINEER: Trevor Butler, trevor.butler@archineers.com
- ICF SUPPLIER: Doug Smith, Future Form, www.futureform.ca, doug@bairdbrosltd.com
- BIO FIBER HEMP BUILDER: Mark Faber, Just BioFiber, www.justbiofiber.ca, mark.faber@justbiofiber.com

PRODUCTS & MATERIALS

- Grundfos Solar Powered Well Pump: https://ca.grundfos.com/products/find-product/sqflex1.html
- Amvic ICF Blocks: https://www.amvicsystem.com
- Off-Grid Appliances by Unique Appliances: https://uniqueappliances.com
- DC Plugs for Electronics by Bix Power: https://www.bixpower.com
- Sketchup 3D Software: https://www.sketchup.com

AFTERWORD

After this long and challenging journey to living off-grid in the forest, I understand better what the saying "don't miss the forest for the trees" means. We are surrounded daily by the beauty of our forested property but at times during this build, I became so deeply immersed in the details of building that I lost sight of why we came to the forest in the first place. It wasn't to create the highest R-value building envelope, find the best insulating windows, or install an array of solar panels. We came to the forest to discover ourselves.

The wilderness has a way of reflecting back to you the best and worst parts of yourself. I discovered my deepest strengths and leaned on them to build the house. In the process, I exposed my worst traits and unconscious fears which at times nearly undermined the entire project. Building a house in the forest was a parable to myself that taught me that I needed to live more in the moment and honor the beauty of my family and the forest that surrounds me daily. Living off-grid is really about reconnecting to your authentic self by detaching from anything that doesn't truly serve your deepest and highest calling.

May the forest be with you.

ABOUT THE AUTHOR

Alvin Tam is not a builder by background — he discovered circus arts as a young adult and ended up performing all over the world with many different productions including the renowned Cirque du Soleil in Las Vegas where he met and married his wife Jada. Together they had a son, and after journeying to Peru to host a yoga retreat, they decided that a more authentic life was calling, with a connection to nature. A few years later, they moved to British Columbia, Canada, bought land and started living off-grid in a 200 square-foot RV without running water. In the meantime, they prepared to build an off-grid house. Having no construction experience, Alvin leaned on the advice of wise builders around him, online videos, and his wits. They now live off-grid in a 1600 square-foot house in the forest, and continue to learn the ways of the wilderness.

MORE FROM US

Barefoot Sanctuary

www.barefootsanctuary.com

Okanagan Yoga and Circus Arts. In the Heart of the Wild.

––––––––

Wolfkin

www.wolfkin.ca

Where Performance Art Meets the Edge of Shamanic Dance

––––––––

Tam Tam Films

www.tamtamfilms.com

Tell Your Story With Us

Printed in Great Britain
by Amazon